Blindness

UNDERSTANDING ILLNESS

Blindness

Elaine Landau

TWENTY-FIRST CENTURY BOOKS

A Division of Henry Holt and Company
New York

Twenty-First Century Books
A Division of Henry Holt and Company, Inc.
115 West 18th Street
New York, NY 10011

Henry Holt ® and colophon are trademarks of
Henry Holt and Company, Inc.
Publishers since 1866

Published in Canada by Fitzhenry & Whiteside Ltd.,
195 Allstate Parkway, Markham, Ontario, L3R 4T8

Library of Congress Cataloging-in-Publication Data
Landau, Elaine.
Blindness / Elaine Landau. — 1st ed.
p. cm. — (Understanding illness)
Includes index.
1. Blindness—Juvenile literature. [1. Blind. 2. Physically
handicapped.] I. Title. II Series: Landau, Elaine.
Understanding illness.
RE52.L36 1994
617.7'12—dc20   94-13832
                                                        CIP
                                                         AC
ISBN 0-8050-2992-3
First Edition 1994

Printed in the United States of America
All first editions are printed on acid-free paper ∞.
10 9 8 7 6 5 4 3 2 1

Photo Credits
p. 12: Perkins School for the Blind; p. 17: Hank Morgan; p. 21: Science
VU/Visuals Unlimited; p. 23: Elena Rooraid/PhotoEdit; p. 27 (left):
Terry Wild Studio; p. 27 (right): Dan McCoy/Rainbow; p. 30: Randy
Kalisek/ F–Stock Inc.; p. 34: David Stoeklein/F–Stock Inc.; p. 37: Scott
Spiker/ F–Stock Inc.; p. 42: Ben Klaffke; pp. 45, 52: International
Association of Lions Clubs; p. 47: New Eyes for the Needy; p. 54: Peter
Byron Photo.

Diagrams on page 15 courtesy of Coherent, Palo Alto, California.

For Michael Brent Pearl

CONTENTS

Blindness

CHAPTER ONE

Being Blind

At 13 Marc had often been told he was lucky to be alive. While innocently walking home from school four years earlier, he was struck in the head by a bullet during a gunfire exchange between neighborhood rival gangs. Although Marc was rushed to the hospital and operated on for several hours, his chances for survival seemed doubtful.

What happened to Marc is not unusual. The involvement of innocent bystanders has become a common trait of America's rising tide of violence. As gangs take root in even small towns and suburbs, potent modern weaponry and random slaughter have taken a serious toll.

However, Marc beat the odds and pulled through. Yet even before he left the hospital, it was obvious that the road ahead would not be easy for him. Violence has become the leading cause of eye injury in the United States, and Marc's gunshot wound left him blind as well as facing other physical challenges.

Marc admits that at first there were days when he wished he had died. His rehabilitation was tedious and difficult. Marc had to deal with considerable pain while recovering and he was often angered and frustrated over having to relearn things he'd mastered as a small child.

*A young blind student enjoying himself
at an outdoor festival.*

Since Marc's medical problems resulted from an unexpected shooting rather than an ongoing illness, he'd never had an opportunity to adjust to what lay ahead. Marc hated being different and he often felt as though he'd been transformed from a promising student and athlete into a "blind kid" overnight.

Yet after spending some time with a counselor, Marc realized that even though the bullet had ripped his tissue and bone, he could stop it from tearing him apart as a human being. Trying to improve the situation, Marc channeled his energy and drive into being all he was before he was shot. Marc learned Braille and resumed his status as a high-achieving student. He intends to go to college after graduating from high school. Through working with a group for blind people, he's also learned to do things he thought he'd never do again. Marc travels independently and handles money, which allows him to shop for himself. Marc also redeveloped senses he once took for granted. His sense of smell became useful in both preparing food and pinpointing locations characterized by a distinct aroma. Marc even claims that in some ways he actually "sees" things more clearly than before.

Marc was also still able to keep in good physical shape by working out in the gym. While some of his friends felt uncomfortable around him, others provided the encouragement and support he needed. Marc made new friends as well.

The blind teenager had simply refused to live life on the sidelines. While he says that it's still sometimes difficult to cope and adapt, he's made remarkable progress. It took time, courage, and determination, but Marc is back in the mainstream and that's where he intends to stay.

CHAPTER TWO

The Causes of Blindness

Marc's case is not as rare as some would believe. According to the National Eye Institute in Bethesda, Maryland, more than 890,000 Americans have severely impaired vision. Ten percent of these individuals are totally blind.

There are numerous causes of blindness and impaired vision. But before we can understand blindness, it's important to know how the eye works. The eye is frequently compared to a camera. Light strikes an object within a person's visual range and that image is reflected to the eye. The light rays travel through the cornea (the clear front window of the eye) and the aqueous humor (the watery fluid behind it). They continue through the pupil (the opening in the colored portion of the eye known as the iris), the lens (the clear disk in the middle of the eye), and the colorless jellylike material behind the lens known as the vitreous humor.

Like a camera, both the cornea and lens focus the light on the retina—the deepest layer of the eye. The retina contains millions of cone- and rod-shaped light sensitive cells that extend to form the optic nerve. The optic nerve sends the image from the retina to the brain. The

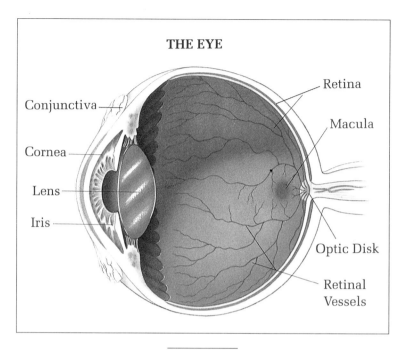

THE EYE

Conjunctiva

Cornea

Lens

Iris

Retina

Macula

Optic Disk

Retinal Vessels

For the human eye to function properly, its components must be in good working order.

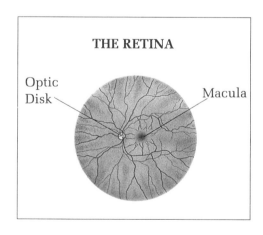

THE RETINA

Optic Disk

Macula

The retina contains about 120 million rods and 6 millon cones.

brain interprets this "visual message" so we recognize what we see.

Many disorders can affect the eye. Unfortunately some may result in severely reduced vision or blindness. Several of the more common ones are described below.

GLAUCOMA

Although glaucoma affects a large number of people throughout the world, the public knows surprisingly little about it. Within the last ten years more than 70,000 Americans have been blinded by glaucoma while another 200,000 lost sight in one eye as a result of it. An additional eight million people are at risk of becoming visually impaired due to glaucoma. Glaucoma is presently the second leading cause of blindness in the United States.

While glaucoma can occur from birth through old age, it is more common among older individuals. The National Association for the Visually Handicapped cites the following conditions and illnesses as special risk factors for glaucoma:

- A family history of glaucoma. Usually more than one person in the family has this disorder.
- Being nearsighted (myopic). Individuals who see well close-up but need corrective glasses or contact lenses to see clearly at a distance are more likely to have glaucoma.
- Diabetes. A high percentage of diabetics eventually have glaucoma.

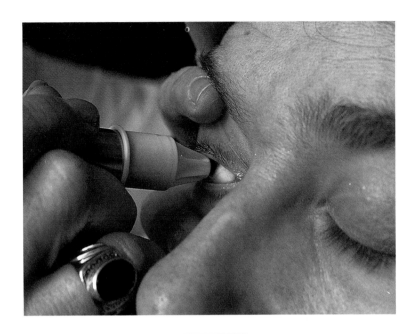

One way to test for glaucoma is by measuring the pressure as more liquid is produced.

- Someone who's had previous eye surgery or an eye injury is at higher risk for glaucoma.
- Individuals suffering from high blood pressure are more likely to have glaucoma.
- African-Americans seem more likely to have glaucoma than whites. The condition also tends to occur at an earlier age and be more severe among them.
- Using steroids for prolonged periods increases an individual's chances of having glaucoma.[1]

Glaucoma may strike in several different ways. This disorder raises pressure in the eye, which can lead to blindness. In most glaucoma cases the aqueous humor (the fluid that nourishes the cornea and lens) becomes blocked. When this liquid is inhibited from draining from the eye, the pressure within the eye mounts as more fluid is produced. This heightened pressure results in damage to the optic nerve and a loss of vision.

All types of glaucoma must be recognized and treated early in order to prevent blindness. Some of the more common forms of glaucoma are discussed below.

PRIMARY OPEN-ANGLE GLAUCOMA

Primary open-angle glaucoma is painless—its only symptom is a gradual loss of vision. At first the person develops blind spots that tend to affect his or her peripheral, or side, vision. Since central vision isn't immediately affected, people often don't even realize they're going blind until much of their sight is gone. Because the disease frequently occurs in older people, the American Academy of Ophthalmology recommends that everyone over 40 have a complete eye exam including an eye pressure check each year. The association further suggests that eye pressure monitoring be a part of routine examinations for all adults as well as children.

If this form of glaucoma is diagnosed early, further vision loss may sometimes be avoided through the use of eyedrops and other medications. At times either traditional or laser surgery may also be necessary. Lasers are used to stretch the drainage channels, allowing for better drainage. If this measure doesn't work, surgery to create an external drain may be successful. However, vision already lost as the result of primary open-angle glaucoma can never be restored.

ACUTE ANGLE-CLOSURE GLAUCOMA

Acute angle-closure glaucoma tends to occur in individuals who have an abnormality in the eye's structure. Unlike primary open-angle glaucoma, which produces a gradual loss of vision, this form of the disease may come on in what's sometimes called a glaucoma attack. There is severe pain and blurred vision, and the person's eye becomes red and irritated.

These episodes must be considered medical emergencies and require immediate attention. The attacks are treated with medication to relieve the pressure in the eye, followed by laser or other surgery to prevent future attacks. If one eye is affected, often the other will also develop the same problem. Therefore laser treatment on both eyes is frequently recommended. The laser creates a hole in the iris and opens and deepens the angle for drainage. If the procedure isn't performed quickly enough, adhesions may develop, permanently sealing the angle. However, with prompt and effective treatment this form of glaucoma can be remedied.

Some individuals suffering from acute angle-closure glaucoma never experience a full-blown attack. Instead they may have several minor attacks or never have an attack at all. This condition is known as chronic angle-closure glaucoma and as in primary open-angle glaucoma, the only signs of its onset are a gradual loss of vision and at times seeing rainbow-colored halos surrounding lighted objects.

Frequently, eye doctors can pinpoint individuals

prone to angle-closure glaucoma by the narrow width of the eye's angle. The tendency toward this eye shape may be hereditary and at times several family members may be affected.

Angle-closure glaucoma is also more common among some ethnic groups than others. It occurs at an extremely high rate among Eskimos in Greenland but is nearly nonexistent in the aborigines of Australia. In the United States primary open-angle glaucoma is the more common form of the disorder, but in many Far Eastern countries angle-closure glaucoma is far more widespread.

Congenital Glaucoma

In this form of the disorder an infant is born with glaucoma. The affected baby's eyes are enlarged, irritated, and watery during the first six months of life. If surgery isn't performed before the condition advances, the child is likely to go blind.

CATARACTS

A cataract is a clouding of the eye's normally clear lens. The degree of cloudiness or opaqueness varies according to how far the cataract has progressed. At first there may be only a light haziness that barely interferes with the person's vision. But at an advanced stage, dense clouding severely limits sight.

Except for protecting their eyes from excessive ultraviolet radiation there is very little healthy individuals can do to prevent cataracts or to stop them from worsening with time. Exercise, diet, and medication will not help the problem. Presently the only treatment available

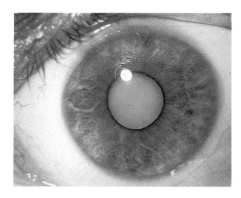

*Here a cataract
has grown over
the lens, inhibiting
the person's sight.
The spot on the
lens is a reflection
from a light.*

is surgery. In cataract surgery the cloudy lens is removed
and usually permanently replaced with a plastic lens.

Patients having cataract surgery generally do not
stay in the hospital overnight but go home soon after the
procedure. If there are no complications, the patient can
usually resume normal daily activities within a short
period of time. Cataract surgery has an extremely high
success rate—nearly 95 percent of the patients have their
vision restored. However, in some cases the existence of
other eye problems makes it impossible to fully restore
the patient's sight.

While we tend to think of cataracts as afflicting the
elderly, infants and children can be affected as well. At
times infants are born with cataracts. In these situations
the cataracts may be hereditary or occur as a result of an
illness the mother suffered during the first three months
of pregnancy, such as German measles.

Other times cataracts develop during childhood due
to an eye injury or even a disease affecting the eye or
another part of the body. In some children cataracts also
appear as the result of abnormal lens growth. Unlike

cataracts in adults, often childhood cataracts only partially cloud the eye's lens. These small cataracts frequently don't affect the young person's vision. Although they should be monitored by an eye doctor, they generally aren't treated. Larger cataracts in children may either be treated with glasses or require surgery.

MACULAR DEGENERATION

Macular degeneration refers to a disorder of the macula— an area at the center of the eye's retina. The macula is responsible for our central vision, which allows us to see clear images of objects, road charts, and books. The progressive, or ongoing, deterioration of the macula may result in a severe loss of central vision but will not lead to total blindness. That's because peripheral, or side, vision is unaffected by the macula.

Although macular degeneration usually affects older individuals, it can appear at any time from birth on. The disorder can be triggered by a number of causes, including an inherited tendency and aging. It may also occur as a result of inflammations, vascular diseases, or drugs affecting the body. Since macular degeneration is so common among elderly people, scientists also believe that it may be linked to the aging process in some way.

The degree of vision loss depends on how far the disorder has progressed. At first the affected individual's central vision may be only slightly blurred, but in time it may be severely impaired. This means that the person may find it extremely difficult to read fine print, do crafts or handiwork that requires attention to detail, or recognize even familiar people or landmarks from a distance.

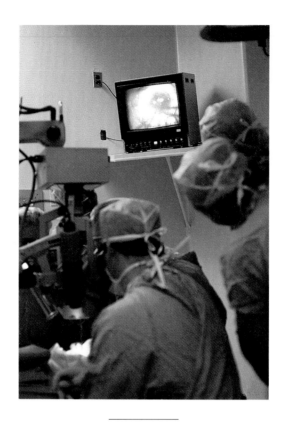

*Due to advances in technology,
ophthalmologists are able to view
a patient's eye on a video screen.*

Since the disorder does not affect peripheral vision, most people with macular degeneration remain independent. Adjusting to the vision loss can be made easier through the use of visual aids such as large-print books and magnifying glasses. The National Eye Institute in Bethesda, Maryland, is presently conducting research at a number of university medical centers to learn more about the possible causes and control of macular problems.

AMBLYOPIA

Amblyopia, sometimes called lazy eye, is a condition in which an eye's vision is limited due to insufficient use during the first three to four years of life. Amblyopia may result from a number of factors. Most commonly the child had convergent strabismus, cross-eyes, while in other situations one eye focused better than the other. Either way one eye develops normal central vision while the other does not.

Amblyopia requires prompt treatment to fully stimulate the weaker eye. If the condition is allowed to continue past the child's third or fourth birthday, its effects are less likely to be reversed. Therefore everyone should be alert to the warning signs that could mean a possible vision problem in young children. These include

- tilting the head to one side to better focus on an object,
- rubbing eyes when not tired,
- closing or partially closing the weaker eye much of the time,
- continually blinking or squinting,
- holding an object unusually close to observe,
- a white spot appearing in the eye's pupil,
- having cross-eyes.

Treatment of amblyopia varies according to the cause of the condition in each child. In cases where the young person's focusing needs improvement, glasses and eye exercises may be prescribed. At times surgery on the person's eye muscles may be necessary. In addition to trying to correct the underlying cause, it's important to also strengthen the weak eye. To accomplish this, a technique known as patching is employed. Patching involves placing a patch over the young person's good eye. This way the weak eye is forced to be stimulated.

DIABETIC RETINOPATHY

One of the negative side effects of diabetes can be vision loss. People who have diabetes are considered 25 times more likely to experience eye problems than those who do not have the illness, and unfortunately diabetes has become the leading cause of adult blindness in the United States. Each year approximately 6,000 new cases of diabetes-related blindness are reported. The longer a person has diabetes, the more likely his or her eyes are to be affected. Nearly 90 percent of people with diabetes who have had the disease for ten years or more experience some eye problems.

Diabetic retinopathy is among the most common and serious eye conditions resulting from diabetes. It occurs when the small blood vessels nourishing the retina deteriorate, resulting in damage to the retina. The effects of this condition vary. The different phases of diabetic retinopathy are as follows:

BACKGROUND RETINOPATHY
(Nonproliferative Retinopathy)
This is the earliest and mildest stage of the condition. At this point the blood vessels in the retina have become blocked and swollen. They may mushroom into small

sacs that spill fluid into the retina, causing swelling and irritation.

Many people with diabetes never have the disease pass beyond this stage. In such instances the individuals might not even notice any distinct eyesight change.

MACULAR EDEMA

(Diabetic Maculopathy)

Some people with diabetic retinopathy suffer more extensive damage. In many of these cases the disease has progressed to a stage known as macular edema, in which the fluid leaking from the blood vessels collects at the macula in the center of the retina. People with macular edema may experience the following:

- blurred reading vision that cannot be corrected with glasses,
- difficulty driving after dark,
- distorted (incorrectly seen) color vision.

While these symptoms can be difficult to deal with, macular edema rarely results in complete blindness.

PROLIFERATIVE RETINOPATHY

This is the most advanced and potentially debilitating form of diabetic retinopathy since it can result in total blindness. At this point small new blood vessels emerge on the retina and optic nerve. These vessels are extremely fragile and bleed easily. Blood spilling from these weakened vessels stops the light from reaching the retina and makes it impossible for the person to see. At times

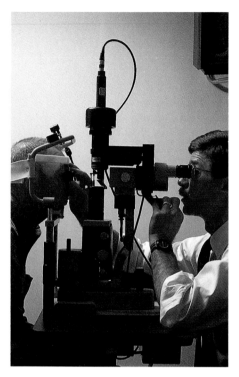
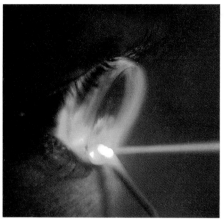

Laser treatment can be used to prevent further loss of vision in diabetic retinopathy. Here a laser is fired through the lens into the retina.

scar tissue forms near the retina during this stage which can cause the retina to detach.

Unfortunately diabetic retinopathy may be difficult to detect since there are no early warning symptoms. Therefore all people with diabetes should have yearly eye examinations. In addition, the Juvenile Diabetes Foundation International/The Diabetic Research Foundation suggests that people with diabetes report any of the following signs to their eye doctor:

- blurry vision,
- double vision,

- a narrowed vision field,
- seeing small floating spots or flakes,
- eye pressure or pain.

It is important to remember that having any or all of the above symptoms does not necessarily mean that the person is suffering from diabetic retinopathy.

Since the 1970s important strides have been made in treating diabetic retinopathy. Although in some cases traditional surgery is required, often laser microsurgery has been used to reduce possible vision loss. A powerful laser beam is aimed at various spots in the retina to seal the leakage in the eye caused by new blood vessels. This form of microsurgery also prevents additional fragile blood vessels from developing.

OTHER CAUSES OF BLINDNESS

Besides the disorders discussed here, and the numerous others that occur, blindness can also be caused by birth defects. In recent years new medical advances have allowed premature infants to live who never would have survived in the past. But unfortunately a significant number of these children are blind or have severely impaired vision. Many people are also blinded as a result of an eye injury, which can occur at any age.

Preventing Blindness

While in some cases blindness may be unavoidable, in many instances it can be prevented through proper precautions and safeguards. Besides disease, numerous injuries can permanently damage our eyes. According to the National Society to Prevent Blindness, 90 percent of all eye injuries can be avoided.

Often accidents that affect the eyes involve children colliding with everyday objects at home. The U.S. Consumer Product Safety Commission estimates that more than 290,000 such incidents occur each year. Some of the most common causes of childhood eye injuries are listed below:

- playing with toys that were meant for older children or that have sharp uncovered edges or shooting parts. Toys that fly, as well as projectile firing toys such as BB guns, are among the worst culprits.
- falls in which the eye is struck by a pointed furniture edge or toy that wasn't put away,
- using potentially dangerous household objects such as pencils, pens, silverware, or fireplace pokers as toys or props in games,

This is a dangerous toy and a potential
lethal weapon in the hands of a young person.

- exposure to pesticides or household chemicals and disinfectants that can be hazardous to eyes.

Often tragic results can be prevented by following some simple safety measures. Young children need to be adequately supervised and given age-appropriate playthings. Homes also must be "childproofed" so that hard surfaces are properly cushioned and sharp objects as well as household and lawn chemicals are safely put away. If dangerous tools or equipment are used in a workshop or home, children must be kept at a safe distance.

Eye injuries among young people also frequently occur during sporting activities and other recreational pastimes. Every year approximately 40,000 sports-related eye injuries are treated in hospital emergency rooms across the nation. However, the true number of these injuries may actually be two to three times as high. That's because this figure does not take into account the injuries treated in physicians' offices or the very severe eye accidents that require immediate hospitalization.

Young athletes should be aware that the sports in which eye injuries are common include baseball, basketball, football, soccer, hockey, boxing, volleyball, and racket sports such as squash, racquetball, paddleball, badminton, and tennis. According to the National Society to Prevent Blindness, baseball injuries most often occur among 5- to 14-year-olds, while basketball injuries are most common among those between 15 and 24 years of age.

While many sports-related eye injuries can be remedied, some result in permanent vision loss. Such eye injuries can also leave the individual more vulnerable to other debilitating eye conditions such as glaucoma and cataracts.

The likelihood of injuring or damaging your eyes while playing a sport depends on a number of factors. Activities that lack aggressive bodily contact or do not have a ball hit another object (bat, racket, foot, hand) pose the least danger to your eyes. These sports include swimming, track and field, and jogging. The sports that pose the greatest risk of eye injury are those with a high degree of combative physical contact such as boxing.

Another eye safety factor in sports is the player's ability. While good balance and coordination and quick reactions are important athletic skills, these are not always well developed in young players. Therefore at times young athletes may be more vulnerable to eye injury than older, more experienced participants. Athletes particularly at risk for serious eye injury are those with preexisting eye conditions that could be worsened as the result of further damage.

If an eye injury occurs while a person is playing a sport, it's important that he or she secure immediate medical attention. Someone unsure as to whether or not the eye has been seriously hurt should have it examined by an eye doctor. The National Society to Prevent Blindness has identified the following conditions among others as signs of possible eye injury:

- fuzzy, blurred vision that does not improve after blinking,
- reduction of the person's normal range of vision,
- sharp or throbbing pain around the eye,
- double vision,
- foreign matter on the eye's cornea,
- cut, scratched, or punctured eye,
- an eye that does not move as fully or easily as the other,
- unusual size or shape of the eye's pupil,
- a layer of blood between the eye's cornea and the iris (the colored circular portion of the eye in front of the lens).

A vast number of eye injuries could be prevented if those involved in sports used protective devices for their eyes and faces. A good example is the case of Stevie Korey, who was injured on his ninth birthday while taking practice swings in a baseball batting cage at his own party. After his turn the young boy merely stepped away from his batting position. He never saw the discharge machine shoot out the extra ball that hit him squarely in the face at a speed of 90 miles an hour. It was a painful, frightening experience that nearly cost the boy his eye.

"Even though Stevie was wearing a regular batting helmet, nothing protected his eyes," his father recalled. "Stevie suffered a detached retina in his right eye as a result. Ten days later Stevie had surgery to reattach the retina. . . . The injury was serious enough that if Stevie hadn't been treated right away, he may have lost far more vision." The boy's mother added, "We thought the regular batting helmet Stevie was wearing was protection enough. If he had worn a face guard or other eye protection, he would have escaped injury."[1]

A year after the accident, Stevie's central vision had been almost fully restored. However, his peripheral vision remained partially limited. He still participates in a number of sports but now wears goggles when doing so.

Fourteen-year-old Jay Eubanks also suffered an eye injury while playing baseball. Jay was pitching in a summer game when a batter slammed a ball directly into his face before he was able to duck. The shattered bones surrounding his right eye socket had to be replaced with titanium plates. By the following summer Jay still hadn't regained total sensation around the injured eye. Despite his injury the teen still dreams of one day playing professional baseball. But to help make his dream come true Jay also wears eye protectors on the ball field.

It's important for athletes of all ages to wear sports eye guards. Sports eye guards come in a wide array of sizes, shapes, and colors, and should fit the user secure-

*An appropriate helmet and eye guards
should be worn when engaging in many sports.*

ly yet comfortably. The eye guards may be used alone in
sports requiring a racket, basketball, and soccer as well as
with a helmet when playing football, hockey, and baseball.

Presently eye guards generally cost between $20 and
$30. For those who wear glasses, eye guards with pre-
scription lenses usually sell for upwards of $60. The fol-
lowing tips for purchasing sports eye protectors have
been recommended by the National Society to Prevent
Blindness:

• Individuals who wear glasses or contact lenses should have their prescription eye guards
  professionally fitted by an eye doctor.

- Monocular athletes, or individuals with only one good seeing eye, should wear eye guards when participating in any sport as well as check with their eye doctor to find out what sports they can safely pursue.
- Whenever possible, eye guards should be purchased at an optical store where prescription lenses are sold. If the buyer must go to a sporting goods store, he or she should ask for a salesperson experienced in this area to help with his or her selection. Athletes who wear contact lenses may use them while wearing eye guards. Prescription eyeglasses or sunglasses should not be worn in place of eye guards unless the lenses are made of a special unbreakable material.
- Pass up sports eye guards that don't have lenses in them, since only "lensed" eye guards provide adequate protection for sports participation. If possible, an eye guard should be selected in which the lenses remain stationary. Otherwise, the lenses should pop outward in the event of an accident. A lens that falls in against the eye can be extremely hazardous.
- At times lenses can fog up during a sporting activity. Therefore it's wise to shop around for eye guards that either have an antifog coating or punctured holes for increased ventilation. It may be best to try on both types to see which is the most comfortable.
- Read the printed material that comes with the

eye protector to see if the product has been tested for use in sports. Also make certain that the item is made of polycarbonate material since these eye guards provide the best protection in the event of an accident.

- To prevent the eye guard from cutting into or irritating the user's skin, it should be padded along the brow and bridge of the nose.
- Don't purchase an eye guard without trying it on. Correct size is crucial if the user is to benefit from maximum protection. The eye guard's strap can be adjusted to insure that it's neither too tight nor too loose.

The National Society to Prevent Blindness launched a public awareness campaign to underscore the importance for children to wear proper eye and face protection when playing sports. The organization stresses that it's never too early to begin practicing sports safety. As Dr. Leonard Parver, founding director of the NSPB-affiliated National Eye Trauma System in Washington, D.C., stated, "The kids who started wearing face masks in youth sports because it was required continued to wear them as they grew older."[2]

Accordingly, the National Society to Prevent Blindness has urged various youth sports groups to require participants to use protective eyewear. As a result of such efforts, Little League baseball teams are recommending that their players use face masks and Dixie Baseball now requires that face shields be used.

Unfortunately each year serious eye injuries also occur among young people off the playing field. That's

*Most industrial workers protect
their eyes on the job—the majority of
eye injuries occur at home.*

what happened to 14-year-old Jonathan while he and his older brother were working on a bookshelf for their room in their father's home carpentry workshop. As the two fashioned the furniture piece, a small particle of wood flew into Jonathan's eye, badly scratching it. While in a great deal of pain the teen was taken to the hospital's emergency room. There he learned that he'd come close to partially losing his vision as a result of the accident. The entire incident could have been avoided if he'd worn safety goggles.

Cases like Jonathan's are not rare. According to Dr. Michael Shapiro, director of the eye training service for the University of Illinois at Chicago Eye Center, "More than half of serious eye injuries happen off the job.

Clearly the most frequent type of eye injury that I treat happens when people are doing yard work and auto maintenance. . . . The irony is that people do hobby, yard, and auto chores for enjoyment or to save money. But even a minor eye injury can be costly, not to mention a major inconvenience. It's much easier to think ahead and put on safety glasses."[3]

The following measures are useful safety checks in avoiding eye injuries:

- wear goggles or safety glasses when using lawn or hobby equipment that is potentially dangerous. They also should be worn by anyone spray painting or using a pesticide.
- carefully read and follow instructions and warning labels on tools and chemicals,
- seat belts and shoulder harnesses should always be worn when riding in a car,
- stairs and steps should be well lighted to reduce the possibility of falls and subsequent eye injuries.

Taking the time to follow these precautions may sometimes seem bothersome. But the trouble involved is minor compared with the possible consequences of serious eye injury.

Blindness:
An International Challenge

Unfortunately blindness and severely impaired vision remain a major health concern in much of the world. The World Health Organization of the United Nations estimates that in the least-developed countries the rate of blindness is often 20 times higher than that of industrialized nations like the United States. There are numerous reasons for the tremendous gap. However, two of the major factors are poverty and a lack of information on what's needed to maintain good vision and healthy eyes.

Ironically some of the most pressing problems seem readily correctable at first glance. Among these is the ongoing deficiency or lack of vitamin A in the diets of millions of children around the world. Vitamin A can be readily obtained from such vegetables as spinach, kale, asparagus, mustard greens, and broccoli, among others. Vitamin A is important for young people during their formative years. They need it to grow and develop normally as well as to combat infection.

Vitamin A is also crucial for vision. The human eye needs it to manufacture the chemicals that detect light, allowing us to see. If a child's vitamin A level falls, the lessened chemicals make it difficult for the child to see in dim light. A more severe chemical drop causes the eye to become dry, resulting in corneal damage. In some cases a severe vitamin A deficiency leads to extensive scarring and blindness.

The problem isn't new. At one time blindness due to malnutrition occurred throughout the world. Descriptions of the condition date back 3,500 years to ancient Egypt. Throughout the nineteenth century numerous cases of malnutrition-related blindness were noted among English schoolchildren as well as among orphans in institutions throughout Denmark and France.

Today the problem largely exists in poor nations around the globe. In recent years blinding malnutrition has been identified in India, Indonesia, the Philippines, Bangladesh, Tanzania, Malawi, Kenya, Zambia, Haiti, Guatemala, Peru, and El Salvador. Unfortunately studies have shown that in such areas between a fourth and half of all preschool children suffer from a lack of vitamin A.

Although anyone can be affected by a vitamin A deficiency, young people between one and five years old are especially vulnerable. That's because many childhood illnesses such as measles or respiratory infections as well as a child's normal growth and development increase the body's need for vitamin A. Infants are born with only the vitamin A stored in their livers prior to birth. If they are breast-fed by mothers who also lack this necessary vitamin, the situation can be troublesome. As the child grows older, a serving of dark green leafy vegetables will yield the daily requirement of vitamin A needed. Yet even in regions where these vegetables are available, they do not always reach the children who need them most.

This is partially due to their parents' not being fully informed about the nutritional needs of young people. Often this occurs in countries where communication and transportation systems are nearly nonexistent, making the delivery of basic health services extremely difficult. In addition, many young children do not like greens and simply refuse to eat them.

At times cultural values and beliefs also influence a population's diet. For example, many people in southern India pass up these vegetables because they are considered "poor people's food." Yet the poorer children who eat them tend to be healthier than those who can afford to eat rice instead. This was particularly evident in the refugee camps of Indonesia, where dark green leafy vegetables were a dietary staple. Besides having fewer vision problems, residents also did not experience the boils and other skin problems common among people in the surrounding villages.

In response, government and private agencies have pursued various strategies to improve the situation. At times a processed food item commonly eaten by most of the children in an area is fortified with vitamin A. In Guatemala sugar was fortified, while in Indonesia and the Philippines a cooking ingredient called monosodium glutamate (MSG) was used. While this method is somewhat effective, unfortunately many foods regularly eaten by the targeted groups cannot be easily fortified.

Perhaps the most popular method used to increase vitamin A intake has consisted of administering large oral doses of the vitamin every six months. This is done either through a concentrated spoonful of the vitamin or with a high-dose vitamin A capsule. So far this method has been tried in India, Indonesia, and Bangladesh with positive results. However, there are drawbacks to it. Even though vitamin A is relatively inexpensive, its widespread distribution can be quite costly. While some coun-

*Broccoli, seen
growing here, is
rich in vitamin A.*

tries continue to sponsor these programs, others facing a host of life threatening illnesses frequently use their meager health resource dollars elsewhere.

Nevertheless in numerous regions valuable strides have been achieved. Many countries have developed educational programs to make parents aware of the importance of a proper diet. In places where there are a variety of ethnic groups and several dialects are spoken, the information is printed with explanatory pictures to make it easier to understand. Some areas have launched projects to grow foods rich in vitamin A as well as continued the search for products that can be fortified with it.

Often residents are encouraged to grow their own household vegetable gardens to insure a continuing source of vitamin A. In some areas both government and private agencies have bought and distributed the seeds. Frequently, those taking part in the project are asked to grow at least two plants containing vitamin A and to eat one of them with their children every day. To attract participants, the agencies award prizes to those with the best gardens as well as sponsor cooking demonstrations.

Although the results of these projects are encouraging, many people in underdeveloped countries also have vision problems that are unrelated to diet. Among these are cataracts, and unfortunately often the people who have them don't know that a simple operation can usually restore vision. The United Nations' World Health Organization cites cataracts as the major cause of blindness in India. In fact, cataracts are responsible for between 50 and 90 percent of the cases in some parts of the country. Approximately seven million Indians cannot work because of cataract vision loss in both eyes, while an equal number have impaired vision.

The numbers are nearly the same in other underdeveloped nations. In Kulhuduffushi, an island of the Republic of Maldives in the Indian Ocean, scores of men and women suffer from cataracts. The medical services direly needed by individuals there and in similar places are unavailable for a number of reasons. Often medical personnel trained in eye surgery are scarce and only found at distant locations. For example, Kulhuduffushi residents needing cataract surgery must go to the Republic's capital of Male, where the country's only eye doctor is. Unfortunately the journey to the capital is long and treacherous and involves crossing rough, stormy seas. The trip would be difficult for an able-bodied sighted person, but it is especially hazardous for someone who is blind.

Yet even in places where there are more physicians, health care isn't always readily available. There are more than 6,000 qualified eye surgeons in India, but unfortunately the hospitals lack adequate room to care for all those who could benefit from cataract surgery. Other factors interfere with securing good eye care as well. In many countries people are unaware of the importance of securing prompt treatment for eye illnesses. At times, even when patients were finally able to get help, they often arrived at the clinic too late. The United Nations' World Health Organization also recognizes the "unavailability of simple eye care equipment and a basic lack of training for rural-based nurses" as serious obstacles.[1]

Yet while much more needs to be done, in some developing countries several important steps have been taken to prevent blindness due to eye disorders and diseases. In nations where there may be a million people to every ophthalmologist, these trained eye specialists spend a good deal of their time training and supervising others in the routine aspects of eye care and treatment. This permits larger numbers of people to profit from their knowledge. In the Fiji Islands of the South Pacific nurses are being trained to provide basic and emergency eye care, while in Malawi health care workers are recruited and trained as ophthalmologic assistants. In addition to other duties, ophthalmologic assistants diagnose and treat eye infections and provide first aid in eye emergencies.

Government and private agencies in the Himalayan kingdom of Nepal have joined forces to reduce the many cases of needless blindness common in the more remote areas of the country. There in the small town of Lahan at the foot of Mount Everest an eye hospital has been set up under the Nepal Blindness Program. This medical center, specializing in high-quality cataract surgery, restores vision to scores of blind patients.

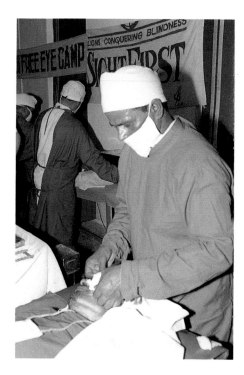

The International Association of Lions Clubs has supported many eye camps in underdeveloped nations.

To reach even greater numbers of people in other areas, "eye camps" have been set up. These are temporary mini-eye hospitals established in schools and other available public buildings. Using thorough sanitation measures, one or two large rooms are turned into operating areas. Eye surgeons and trained surgical nurses are flown in to work at the camps for a day or two. The medical teams operate on as many as 300 cataract patients a day—allowing people to see who would have otherwise remained blind for life. Many patients stay at the eye camps for up to a week following surgery, where they receive the necessary aftercare. They are given free food during their stay as well as free transportation to and from the camp.

At first these pioneering efforts were largely performed by doctors from missions and international health organizations. But once it became obvious that more people were having their eyesight restored at eye camps than in hospitals, a number of governments began to establish similar programs. Often strings of mobile eye camps were set up at countryside locations at predetermined times of the year.

Besides these portable eye hospitals, some developing countries also sponsor eye screening camps. The camps encourage residents to come in for eye testing and treatment. Eye problems are treated and prescriptions for free glasses are given out. If it's determined that the patient needs surgery, he or she can sometimes be transported to the nearest operating facility the same day.

With such rewarding results you may wonder why these efforts have not been duplicated worldwide. However, the mobile eye screening camps and hospitals are not without problems. It's frequently hard to find suitable buildings in which to house these facilities and often quite costly to install the needed equipment and electrical connections for operations. At times it's also difficult to secure the increasing numbers of volunteers necessary to run the camps. Transporting food and sanitary supplies to these sites has become more expensive in recent years as well.

Many other helpful measures have been international in scope. New Eyes for the Needy, as an example, is a New Jersey-based nonprofit volunteer organization dedicated to providing "better vision for the poor the world over." The group sends recycled glasses to people who need them in underdeveloped countries. During 1993–1994 about 175,000 eyeglasses were shipped to India, Africa, Central and South America, and the Caribbean.

A volunteer at New Eyes for the Needy helps recycle glasses to be sent overseas.

New Eyes for the Needy has also assisted people in the United States. More than 3,000 pairs of glasses were purchased with New Eyes funds in 1993 for Americans who could not afford them. The glasses were issued through a voucher system after careful screening at hospitals, clinics, and schools. Over the past 60 years it is estimated that 400,000 people in the United States have benefited by the sight-saving services of New Eyes for the Needy. Donations of glasses have been received from every state in the nation and the group has helped provide glasses for individuals in all 50 states as well. Many of the recipients have been children and teenagers.

Endeavors to prevent blindness and impaired vision in underdeveloped countries and poorer areas of developed countries have made a vast difference in the lives of millions of people. Regardless of the work and costs involved, the human benefits are priceless.

Separating Fact from Fiction

No matter where you live, preserving your eyes involves learning the facts about eye disorders and eye care. Being knowledgeable also enables sighted people to better understand and relate to blind people and those with severely impaired vision. Do you know the answers to the true-or-false questions below?

Eating as many carrots as possible guarantees good vision.

False. Carrots as well as many leafy green vegetables contain vitamin A, which is crucial to good vision. However, the amount of this vitamin needed is present in a well-balanced diet. Taking an excessive amount of vitamin A could actually be harmful rather than beneficial.

Reading print that is extremely small for long periods will permanently damage your eyes.

False. In answer to this question, Dr. Linda Casser, an optometrist and director of the Indianapolis Eye Care Center, noted, "This is one of the most common myths about vision I hear. Many older people especially feel they should not read too much because it will wear out their eyes."[1] Although extensively reading fine print can cause eye fatigue, it does not damage or wear out the human eye.

Reading in poor light will destroy your eyes.
False. As with reading large portions of fine print, reading in improper lighting may cause eye fatigue. However, contrary to the common myth, it will not permanently injure your eyes. But good light will help magnify the print.

Laser surgery can be used to remove cataracts.
False. "Lasers are used successfully in a number of new procedures," stated Dr. Eve J. Higginbotham, an ophthalmologist and associate professor at University of Michigan's W. K. Kellogg Eye Center. "But a cataract, which is a clouded lens of the eye, can only be removed by conventional surgery."[2] Part of the confusion may be due to the fact that in 98 percent of cataract removal procedures the capsule or wrapping that contains the lens is not removed as well. In time the capsule may cloud, causing the person's vision to blur. Laser techniques may be used on the capsule to clear the individual's sight, but this should not be confused with the original cataract surgery.

Children usually outgrow their eye problems and don't need to see a doctor unless the trouble continues into young adulthood.
False. Children's vision problems must be taken seriously. A number of common childhood eye conditions such as strabismus, which is when one eye cannot focus properly, resulting in a squint; convergent strabismus, or

cross-eyes, when one or both eyes turn inward; and amblyopia, lazy eye, need medical treatment to be corrected. In many cases the sooner the problem is taken care of, the better the person's chance for a full recovery. An eye examination by age three is a wise precaution.

You don't need to see an eye doctor unless you've been experiencing eye problems.
False. This belief is particularly dangerous since it can be harmful to maintaining good vision. As one ophthalmologist said, "By the time patients notice signs or symptoms, their eye conditions can be advanced and very hard to control. In many cases, particularly with glaucoma, the damage is irreversible."[3] Having regularly scheduled eye examinations as well as wearing protective eye gear when appropriate can go a long way in preventing blindness and impaired vision.

Someone with a serious eye disorder such as glaucoma, cataracts, or diabetic retinopathy will eventually go blind.
False. Due to medical advances many disorders that once led to total blindness can now be effectively halted. Today affected people are often left with a condition known as low vision. Low vision has sometimes been described as being "a little bit blind," "trying to see through a thin coat of Vaseline," or "viewing the world as if through a narrow tunnel." People with low vision have extremely limited sight that cannot be remedied by even the strongest glasses available.

The major causes of low vision include macular degeneration, glaucoma, diabetic retinopathy, and cataracts. Children as well as adults can be affected. Some young people must contend with low vision as a result of a congenital defect (present at birth) or an eye injury.

While living with low vision can be frustrating, help is available. Some people with low vision have managed to stay on their jobs after making changes in their work area. At times these may include better lighting or reducing the level of glare in an office. A number of clinics and organizations offer a wealth of information and aids to individuals with low vision. These include large-print books, extradark felt-tipped pens, magnifiers either with or without illumination, telescopes that can be built into prescription glasses, and electronic reading systems. There's also computer software capable of enlarging an image more than 50 times its size.

We should pity blind people and let them know how bad we feel for them.

False. Actually nothing could be further from the truth. A blind person does not need your sympathy but should be given the same respect and consideration you'd show a sighted individual. The Lighthouse Inc., an organization dedicated to enabling blind and partially sighted people to lead productive lives, cites the following behaviors as appropriate when interacting with a blind person:

> **On the Street**: Ask if assistance would be helpful. Grabbing an arm or pushing is both dangerous and discourteous. Sometimes a blind person prefers to proceed unaided. If the person wants your help, offer your elbow. As the two of

If help is needed by a blind person, offer your arm and walk slightly ahead of your blind companion.

you continue to walk, you should remain a half step ahead. This way your body movements will indicate when you're about to switch directions or stop and start.

Giving Directions: When providing a blind person with directions use that individual's position as the focal point of your instructions. For example, you might say, "You are facing Knoll Street and you must cross it as you continue west on Cedar Crest Avenue."

Handling Money: When giving bills to a blind person, say what each bill is as you hand it to

him or her. This allows the individual to immediately identify the money and put it away
accordingly.

Safety: Consideration of others is a key in maintaining a safe environment for both sighted and
blind people. Doors left partially open can
prove hazardous to everyone but are especially
so for the blind. Therefore it's important to keep
all doors either completely open or shut.

Dining Out: Offer your arm to guide a blind person to the table. Do not shove the person into a
chair but place his or her hand on the chair's
back so the person can seat him- or herself.
Read the menu aloud and let the waiter speak
directly to the blind person when it's his or her
turn to order. Describe how the food is placed
on the dish as though it were a clock. You might
say, "The peas are at three o'clock, the potatoes
at six o'clock, and the fish at nine o'clock."

Traveling: Both sighted and blind people enjoy
guided tours of new places highlighting points
of interest. When traveling with a blind person
feel free to describe unfamiliar scenery and
sights you feel the person might enjoy hearing
about.

Dog Guides: Dog guides are working animals
with an important job to do. Do not distract
these dogs by calling out to them, petting them,
or offering them food.

*A dog guide assists a blind person
in traveling independently.*

Relating to Blind People: Speak to a blind person the same way you'd talk to anyone else. It's all right to use phrases such as, "See you later," or "Did you see that?" in conversation. If you enter a room in which a blind person is alone, let the person know you're there by speaking or introducing yourself. Be sure to let the blind person know when you're leaving as well.

Yet how you relate to blind people on a more meaningful level is of even greater importance. It's crucial for sighted individuals to try to see clearly—casting off any stereotypical or negative notions they might have about blind people. Everyone profits when each of us is judged as an individual.

Perhaps the best proof of this is the experience of a blind seven-year-old girl attending public school in Ohio. As one of the 130 visually impaired students in her school system, she was the youngest totally blind child ever to go to class alongside sighted students.

Fortunately her second-grade classmates were able to see past her vision problem and enjoy being with her. "She's a regular girl," reported one of her friends, who likes leading her new classmate through hopscotch games. Besides playground activities, the seven-year-old also likes her classroom subjects and especially enjoys stories. Her favorite is "The Little Red Hen," because, as she put it, "It teaches you that if you help friends, they will help you."[4]

E N D
NOTES

CHAPTER 2
1. Andrew M. Prince, M.D., and Gregory K. Harmon, M.D., *Glaucoma: The Sneak Thief of Sight* (New York: NAVH, 1993), 8.

CHAPTER 3
1. "Sports Eye Safety," *Prevent Blindness News*, Summer 1993, 4.

2. Ibid., 5

3. "Home Eye Safety: Is Your Home Hazardous to Your Eyes?" *Prevent Blindness News*, Summer 1993, 5.

CHAPTER 4
1. V. Guy Hawley, "Training Rural-Based Nurses," *World Health*, May 1987, 12.

CHAPTER 5
1. "The Facts on Common Eye Myths," *Prevent Blindness News*, Summer 1993, 1.

2. Ibid.

3. Ibid.

4. "Stepping Out," *Life*, December 1989, 7.

GLOSSARY

amblyopia—a condition also known as lazy eye in which an eye's vision is reduced due to insufficient use during early childhood

aqueous humor—the watery fluid behind the cornea of the eye (*see* cornea)

cataract—a clouding of the usually clear lens of the eye, which eventually results in a loss of vision

cornea—the clear transparent outercoat of the eyeball

diabetic retinopathy—a condition that occurs in people with diabetes when the retina is damaged by the breakdown of small blood vessels that supply it with vitamins and nutrients (*see* retina)

glaucoma—a condition in which pressure in the eye builds up resulting in damage to the optic nerve and a progressive loss of vision

iris—the colored membrane surrounding the eye's pupil (*see* pupil)

laser surgery—a form of microsurgery in which a high-powered laser beam is used. Laser surgery on eyes is frequently performed in a physician's office.

lens—the clear disk in the middle of the eye

macular degeneration—an eye condition resulting in a loss of central vision

optic nerve—a cord of nerve fibers that transmits visual messages from the retina to the brain (*see* retina)

pupil—the circular opening in the iris through which light passes (*see* iris)

retina—the light sensitive membrane coating the back of the eyeball

vascular disease—a condition involving ducts or vessels, such as blood vessels

FURTHER READING

Adler, David A. *A Picture Book of Helen Keller*. New York: Holiday House, 1990.

Alexander, Sally Hobart. *Mom's Best Friend*. New York: Macmillan, 1992.

———*Mom Can't See Me*. New York: Macmillan, 1990.

Arnold, Caroline. *A Guide Dog Puppy Grows Up*. New York: Harcourt Brace Jovanovich, 1991.

Bergman, Thomas. *Seeing in Special Ways: Children Living with Blindness*. Milwaukee: Gareth Stevens Children's Books, 1989.

Krementz, Jill. *How It Feels to Live with a Physical Disability*. New York: Simon & Schuster, 1992.

Smith, Elizabeth Simpson. *A Guide Dog Goes to School: The Story of a Dog Trained to Lead the Blind*. New York: Morrow, 1987.

ORGANIZATONS
CONCERNED WITH BLINDNESS
AND VISION LOSS

American Council of the Blind
1155 15th Street NW, Suite 720
Washington, D.C. 20005

American Foundation for the Blind
15 West 16th Street
New York, NY 10011

Associated Services for the Blind
919 Walnut Street
Philadelphia, PA 19107

Blind Children's Fund
230 Central Street
Auburndale, MA 02166

Council of Families with Visual Impairment
14400 Cedar Road, Apt. 108
University Heights, OH 44121

Helen Keller International
15 West 16th Street
New York, NY 10011

International Guiding Eyes
13445 Glenoaks Blvd.
Sylmar, CA 91342

Jewish Guild for the Blind
15 West 65th Street
New York, NY 10023

The Lighthouse Inc.
111 East 59th Street
New York, NY 10022

**National Association for Parents
of the Visually Impaired**
2180 Linway
Beloit, WI 53511

National Federation of the Blind
1800 Johnson Street
Baltimore, MD 21230

National Society to Prevent Blindness
500 East Remington Road
Schaumburg, IL 60173

New Eyes for the Needy, Inc.
549 Millburn Avenue
Short Hills, NJ 07078

Recording for the Blind
20 Roszel Road
Princeton, NJ 08540

The Seeing Eye
P. O. Box 375
Morristown, NJ 07963-0375

INDEX